THE OFFICIAL
FORMULAONE
ANNUAL 2010

Written by David Clayton
Designed by Simon Thorley

GRANADA

Ventures

The ITV Sport logo is licensed by Granada Ventures Ltd.
All rights reserved.

A Grange Publication

© 2009. Published by Grange Communications Ltd., Edinburgh, under licence from Granada Ventures Ltd. Printed in the EU.

ISBN 978-1-906211-94-3

£6.99

CONTENTS

FACTS&FIGURES

The 2008 Formula One championship was one of the most exciting in the history of the sport with the title going right down to the last race – it was dramatic, controversial and summed up why F1 is perhaps the greatest spectator sport on the planet. Best of all, it was won by Britain's Lewis Hamilton – here are the top three finishes of all 18 races…

AUSTRALIA – MARCH 16TH 2008 – MELBOURNE GRAND PRIX CIRCUIT
1. Lewis Hamilton - McLaren
2. Nick Heidfeld – BMW Sauber
3. Nico Rosberg – Williams

MALAYSIA – MARCH 23RD 2008 – SEPANG INTERNATIONAL CIRCUIT
1. Kimi Räikkönen – Ferrari
2. Robert Kubica – BMW Sauber
3. Heikki Kovalainen – McLaren

BAHRAIN – APRIL 6TH 2008 – BAHRAIN INTERNATIONAL CIRCUIT
1. Felipe Massa – Ferrari
2. Kimi Räikkönen – Ferrari
3. Robert Kubica – BMW Sauber

SPAIN – APRIL 27TH 2008 – CIRCUIT DE CATALUNYA
1. Kimi Räikkönen – Ferrari
2. Felipe Massa – Ferrari
3. Lewis Hamilton – McLaren

TURKEY – MAY 11TH 2008 – ISTANBUL RACING CIRCUIT
1. Felipe Massa – Ferrari
2. Lewis Hamilton – McLaren
3. Kimi Räikkönen – Ferrari

MONACO – MAY 25TH 2008 – CIRCUIT DE MONACO
1. Lewis Hamilton – McLaren
2. Robert Kubica – BMW Sauber
3. Felipe Massa – Ferrari

CANADA – JUNE 8TH 2008 – CIRCUIT GILLES VILLENEUVE
1. Robert Kubica – BMW Sauber
2. Nick Heidfeld – BMW Sauber
3. David Coulthard – Red Bull

FRANCE – JUNE 22ND 2008 – CIRCUIT DE NEVERS MAGNY-COURS
1. Felipe Massa – Ferrari
2. Kimi Räikkönen – Ferrari
3. Jarno Trulli – Toyota

BRITAIN – JULY 6TH 2008 – SILVERSTONE CIRCUIT
1. Lewis Hamilton – McLaren
2. Nick Heidfeld – BMW Sauber
3. Rubens Barrichello – Honda

GERMANY – JULY 20TH 2008 – HOCKENHEIMRING
1. Lewis Hamilton – McLaren
2. Nelsinho Piquet – Renault
3. Felipe Massa – Ferrari

HUNGARY – AUGUST 3RD 2008 – HUNGARORING
1. Heikki Kovalainen – McLaren
2. Timo Glock – Toyota
3. Kimi Räikkönen – Ferrari

EUROPEAN – AUGUST 24TH 2008 – VALENCIA STREET CIRCUIT
1. Felipe Massa – Ferrari
2. Lewis Hamilton – McLaren
3. Robert Kubica – BMW Sauber

BELGIUM – SEPTEMBER 7TH 2008 – CIRCUIT DE SPA-FRANCORCHAMPS
1. Felipe Massa – Ferrari
2. Nick Heidfeld – BMW Sauber
3. Lewis Hamilton – McLaren

ITALY – SEPTEMBER 14TH 2008 – AUTODROMO NAZIONALE MONZA
1. Sebastian Vettel – Toro Rosso
2. Heikki Kovalainen – McLaren
3. Robert Kubica – BMW Sauber

**SINGAPORE – SEPTEMBER 28TH 2008
– MARINA BAY**

1.   Fernando Alonso – Renault
2.   Nico Rosberg – Williams
3.   Lewis Hamilton – McLaren

**JAPAN – OCTOBER 12TH 2008 –
FUJI SPEEDWAY**

1.   Fernando Alonso – Renault
2.   Robert Kubica – BMW Sauber
3.   Kimi Räikkönen – Ferrari

**CHINA – OCTOBER 19TH 2008 –
SHANGHAI INTERNATIONAL CIRCUIT**

1.   Lewis Hamilton – McLaren
2.   Felipe Massa – Ferrari
3.   Kimi Räikkönen – Ferrari

**BRAZIL – NOVEMBER 2ND 2008 -
AUTÓDROMO JOSÉ CARLOS PACE**

1.   Felipe Massa – Ferrari
2.   Fernando Alonso – Renault
3.   Kimi Räikkönen – Ferrari

FACTS&FIGURES

Placing	Driver	Team	Po
1st	Lewis Hamilton	McLaren	98
2nd	Felipe Massa	Ferrari	97
3rd	Kimi Räikkönen	Ferrari	75
4th	Robert Kubica	BMW Sauber	75
5th	Fernando Alonso	Renault	61
6th	Nick Heidfeld	BMW Sauber	60
7th	Heikki Kovalainen	McLaren	53
8th	Sebastian Vettel	Toro Rosso	35
9th	Jarno Trulli	Toyota	31
10th	Timo Glock	Toyota	25
11th	Mark Webber	Red Bull	21
12th	Nelsinho Piquet	Renault	19
13th	Nico Rosberg	Williams	17
14th	Rubens Barrichello	Honda	11
15th	Kazuki Nakajima	Williams	9
16th	David Coulthard	Red Bull	8
17th	Sébastien Bourdais	Toro Rosso	4
18th	Jenson Button	Honda	3
19th	Giancarlo Fisichella	Force India	0
20th	Adrian Sutil	Force India	0
21st	Takuma Sato	Super Aguri	0
22nd	Anthony Davidson	Super Aguri	0

CONSTRUCTORS' CHAMPIONSHIP 2008

Placing	Team	Engine	Wins	Po
1st	Ferrari	Ferrari	8	17
2nd	McLaren	Mercedes	6	15
3rd	BMW Sauber	BMW	1	13
4th	Renault	Renault	2	80
5th	Toyota	Toyota	0	56
6th	Toro Rosso	Ferrari	1	39
7th	Red Bull	Renault	0	29
8th	Williams	Toyota	0	26
9th	Honda	Honda	0	14
10th	Force India	Ferrari	0	0
11th	Super Aguri	Honda	0	0

AUSTRALIAN GRAND PRIX

ALBERT PARK, MELBOURNE

First Race: 1996
Circuit Length: 5.272 Km
Laps: 58
Built: 1996
Capacity: 80,000

MALAYSIAN GRAND PRIX

SEPANG INTERNATIONAL CIRCUIT, KUALA LUMPAR

First Race: 1999
Circuit Length: 5.510 Km
Laps: 56
Built: 1998
Capacity: 130,000

CHINESE GRAND PRIX

SHANGHAI CIRCUIT, SHANGHAI

First Race: 2004
Circuit Length: 5.419 Km
Laps: 56
Built: 2003/2004
Capacity: 200,000

BAHRAIN GRAND PRIX

BAHRAIN INTERNATIONAL
RACING CIRCUIT, SAKHIR

First Race: 2004
Circuit Length: 5.381 Km
Laps: 57
Built: 2003/2004
Capacity: 50,000

JENSON BUTTON

Team: Brawn GP
Born: 19/01/1980
Nationality: British
Birthplace: Frome, Somerset UK
World Championships: 0
Highest Finish: 1
Race Wins: 7

RUBENS BARRICHELLO

Team: Brawn GP
Born: 23/05/1972
Nationality: Brazilian
Birthplace: Sao Paulo, Brazil
World Championships: 0
Highest Finish: 1
Race Wins: 9

SEBASTIAN VETTEL

Team: Red Bull
Born: 03/07/1987
Nationality: German
Birthplace: Heppenheim, Germany
World Championships: 0
Highest Finish: 1
Race Wins: 3

MARK WEBBER

Team: Red Bull
Born: 27/08/1976
Nationality: Australian
Birthplace: Queanbeyan, Australia
World Championships: 0
Highest Finish: 1
Race Wins: 1

DETAILS CORRECT TO 31/07/09

SEBASTIANVETTEL

SPOT THE DIFFERENCE

Picture A is different from Picture B – can you find and circle the six changes we've made in Picture B?

Answers on pg 58

SPANISH GRAND PRIX

CIRCUIT DE CATALUNYA, BARCELONA

First Race: 1991
Circuit Length: 4.627 Km
Laps: 66
Built: 1991
Capacity: 67,730

MONACO GRAND PRIX

CIRCUIT DE MONACO, MONTE CARLO

First Race: 1950
Circuit Length: 3.320 Km
Laps: 78
Built: 1950 (street circuit)
Capacity: 50,000

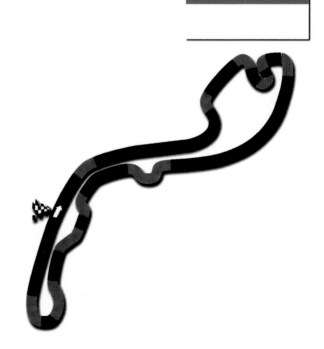

TURKISH GRAND PRIX

ISTANBUL PARK CIRCUIT, ISTANBUL

First Race: 2005
Circuit Length: 5.307 Km
Laps: 58
Built: 2005
Capacity: 155,000

BRITISH GRAND PRIX

SILVERSTONE CIRCUIT, NORTHANTS

First Race: 1950
Circuit Length: 5.110 Km
Laps: 60
Built: 1948
Capacity: 90,000

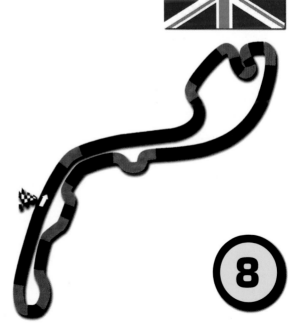

16 THINGS YOU DIDN'T KNOW ABOUT

1 • He was born on the **19 January 1980** in Frome, Somerset UK.

2 • His father is John Button, the former Rallycross driver.

3 • He attended Selwood Middle School and then Frome Community College.

4 • He began karting at age 8 and was very successful by winning all **34 races** of the **1991 British Cadet Karting Championship.**

5 • He then moved on and won Formula Ford aged 18, also winning the Formula Ford Festival.

6 • In 1998 he won the annual McLaren Autosport BRDC Young Driver Award.

7 • As a prize for the McLaren Young Driver Award, he received a test in their F1 car - this was in late 1999 when he was just 19.

8 • In 2000 he started his F1 career with Williams and finished eighth overall.

JENSON BUTTON

9 • In 2001 he moved to Benetton (now Renault) although still under contract with Williams and finished 17th overall.

10 • In 2002 Benetton changed to Renault and he finished seventh.

11 • In 2003 he moved to BAR Honda where he stayed until 2005.

12 • In 2006 BAR Honda changed to Honda and he stayed there until his move to Brawn GP for 2009.

13 • In his spare time he likes mountain biking and body boarding.

14 • He mainly lives in Monaco, France but also has property in the UK and Bahrain.

15 • He has a varied car collection that contains a 1956 VW Campervan, a Bugatti Veyron and a Honda S600.

16 • His first F1 race was at the 2000 Australian Grand Prix.

CIRCUITBREAKER QUIZ

Test your knowledge of the F1 circuits of the world! Below are eight images taken from various F1 venues – see if you can name them all by using detective work and following the clues within the pictures...

Answers on pg 58

JARNO TRULLI

Team: Toyota
Born: 13/07/1974
Nationality: Italian
Birthplace: Pescara, Italy
World Championships: 0
Highest Finish: 1
Race Wins: 1

NICO ROSBERG

Team: Williams
Born: 27/06/1985
Nationality: German
Birthplace: Wiesbaden, Germany
World Championships: 0
Highest Finish: 2
Race Wins: 0

FELIPE
MASSA

Team: Ferrari
Born: 25/04/1981
Nationality: Brazilian
Birthplace: Sao Paulo, Brazil
World Championships: 0
Highest Finish: 1
Race Wins: 11

TIMO
GLOCK

Team: Toyota
Born: 18/03/1982
Nationality: German
Birthplace: Lindenfels, Germany
World Championships: 0
Highest Finish: 2
Race Wins: 0

DETAILS CORRECT TO 31/07/09

GUESS WHO ?

Can you guess which current F1 drivers are below? Look closely for clues, but you may need to dig deep and use detective work to get all four!

Answers on pg 58

THE CAR'S THE STAR

Sometimes things are so simple, we don't pay them any attention. Do you know everything about a Formula One car? If you're unsure, here is the basic info everyone should know...

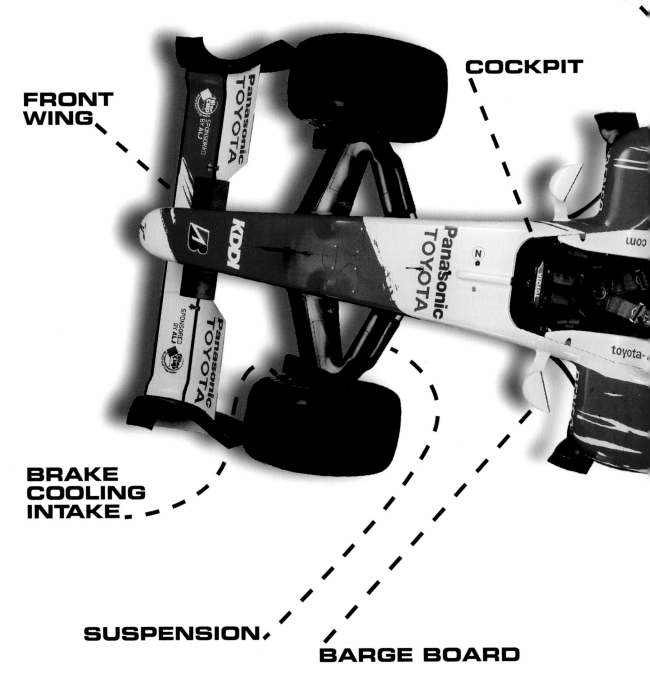

CAMERA MOUNT

COCKPIT

FRONT WING

BRAKE COOLING INTAKE

SUSPENSION

BARGE BOARD

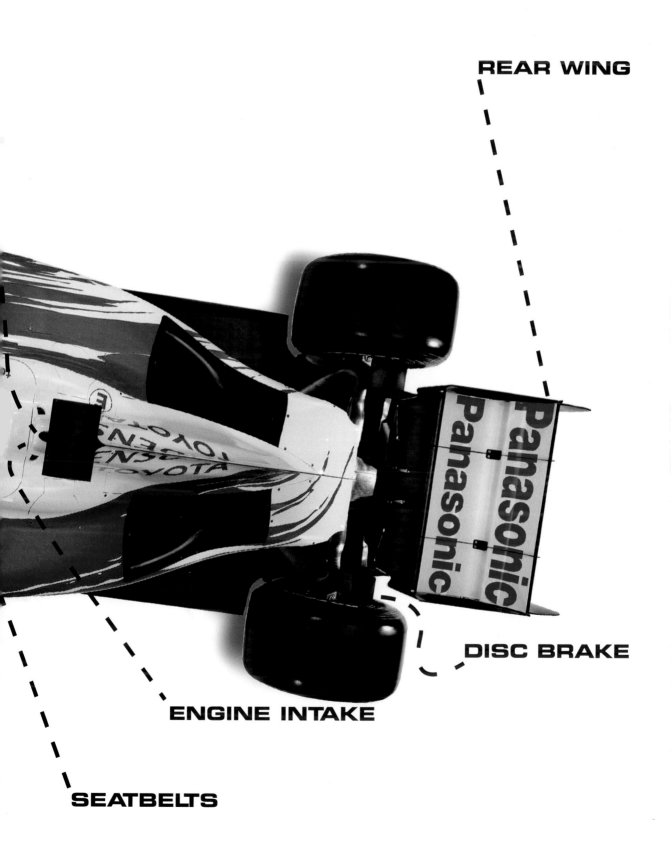

REAR WING

DISC BRAKE

ENGINE INTAKE

SEATBELTS

F1 CROSSWORD

Read the clues, fill in the relevant spaces and see if you can complete the crossword...

ACROSS

04 ___ lane - where the cars are housed and repaired during races? (3)
06 Number of people who raced in the 2009 season? (6)
07 Kimi _____ - the 2007 World Champion? (9)
08 Surname of the 2008 Champion - Lewis _____ ? (8)
10 _____ Button - the first name of the driver who won the 2009 Australian Grand Prix? (6)
14 _____ flag - symbolises the end of a race? (9)
16 Colour of Ferrari's cars? (3)
17 What determines a driver's place on the grid? (10)
18 Safety equipment that drivers wear on their heads? (6)
19 These notify the drivers when to go? (6)

DOWN

01 These red and white stripes are found on corners? (4)
02 If it is not a race circuit, it is a _____ circuit? (6)
03 _____ Senna - christian name of famous driver? (6)
05 Number of points gained for winning a Formula 1 championship race? (3)
09 The place where the Monaco Grand Prix is held? (10)
11 What powers an engine? (4)
12 Where Felipe Massa was born? (6)
13 Legendary racing team that has showcased such talents as Michael Schumacher? (7)
14 Another word for a track? (7)
15 Without one of these the car would not move? (6)

FERNANDO ALONSO

Team: Renault
Born: 29/07/1981
Nationality: Spanish
Birthplace: Oviedo, Spain
World Championships: 2
Highest Finish: 1
Race Wins: 21

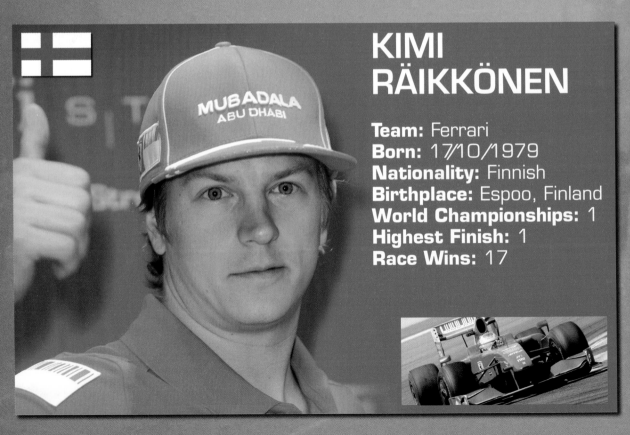

KIMI RÄIKKÖNEN

Team: Ferrari
Born: 17/10/1979
Nationality: Finnish
Birthplace: Espoo, Finland
World Championships: 1
Highest Finish: 1
Race Wins: 17

LEWIS HAMILTON

Team: McLaren
Born: 07/01/1985
Nationality: British
Birthplace: Stevenage, UK
World Championships: 1
Highest Finish: 1
Race Wins: 10

NICK HEIDFELD

Team: BMW Sauber
Born: 10/05/1977
Nationality: German
Birthplace: Monchengladbach, Germany
World Championships: 0
Highest Finish: 2
Race Wins: 0

GERMAN GRAND PRIX

NÜRBURGRING CIRCUIT, NÜRBURG

First Race: 1984
Circuit Length: 5.118 Km
Laps: 60
Built: 1984
Capacity: 400,000

HUNGARIAN GRAND PRIX

HUNGARORING CIRCUIT BUDAPEST

First Race: 1986
Circuit Length: 4.355 Km
Laps: 70
Built: 1986
Capacity: 120,000

EUROPEAN GRAND PRIX (SPAIN)

STREET CIRCUIT, VALENCIA

First Race: 2008
Circuit Length: 5.387 Km
Laps: 57
Built: 2008
Capacity: 112,771

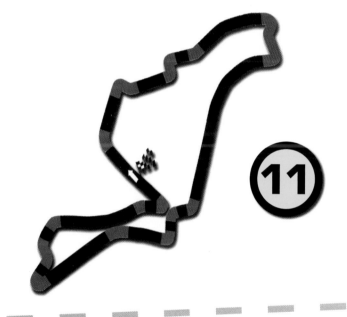

11

BELGIAN GRAND PRIX

SPA FRANCORCHAMPS CIRCUIT, FRANCORCHAMPS

First Race: 1983 (Revised Shorter Version)
Circuit Length: 6.963 Km
Laps: 44
Built: 1924 (street circuit)
Capacity: Approx 90,000

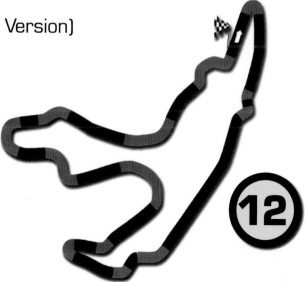

12

WORDSEARCH

Can you find the 10 hidden words connected with a Formula One car? Remember, the words could be concealed in a horizontal, vertical, or diagonal way!

K	N	A	T	L	E	U	F	Y	R
E	L	E	C	T	R	I	C	A	L
B	T	S	G	A	R	D	L	R	W
L	S	E	B	R	A	K	E	S	H
K	U	R	K	D	H	E	K	R	E
B	A	Y	V	W	N	Z	N	P	E
L	H	T	R	I	I	O	R	C	L
Z	X	M	G	L	S	N	T	T	S
D	E	N	J	E	K	K	G	J	C
C	E	Z	G	K	N	T	Y	F	Q

Answers on pg 59

JARNO TRULLI

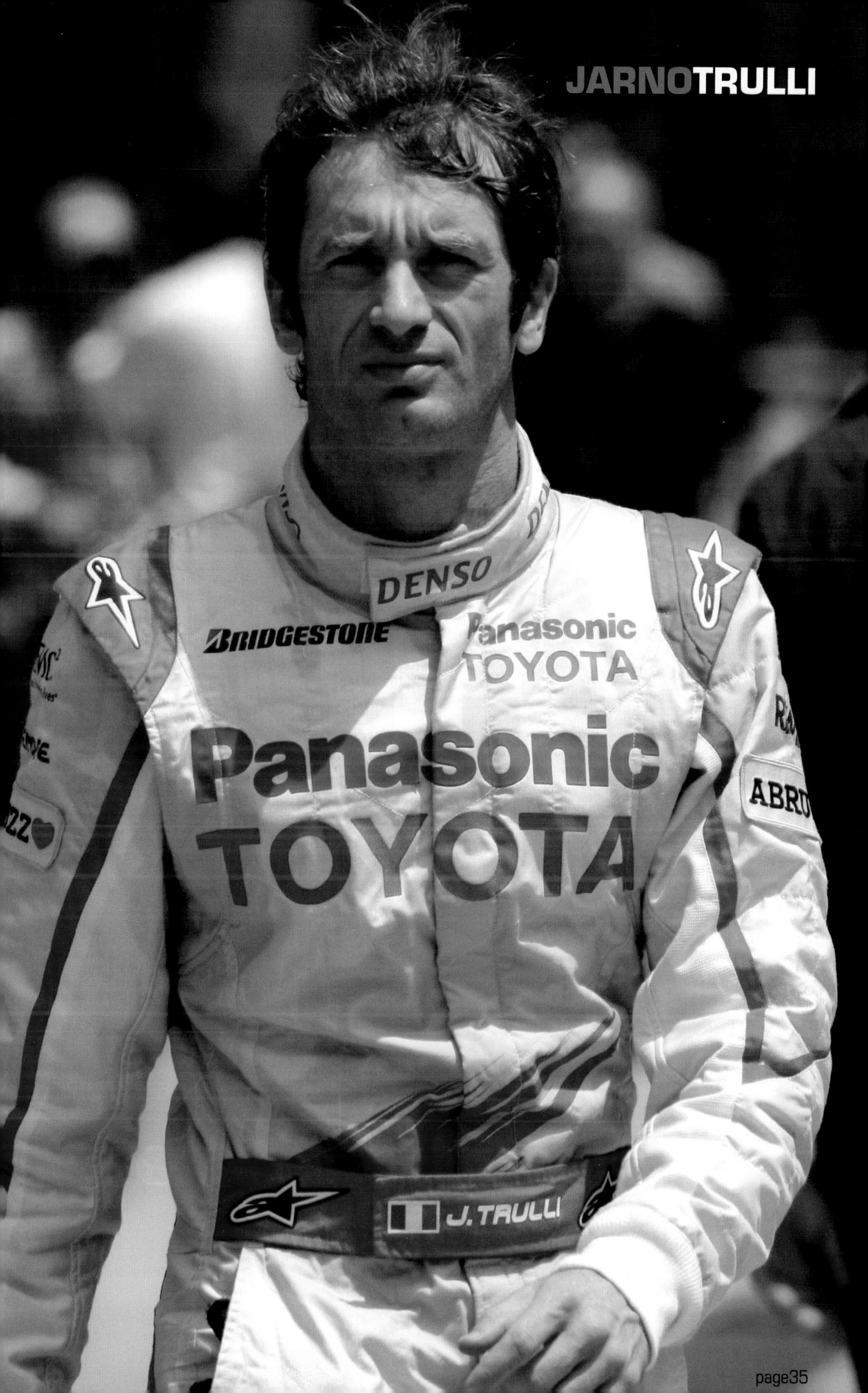

THE BIG F1 QUIZ 2010

Test your knowledge to the full in our high-octane Formula One quiz – let's see how much you really know…

1. How many teams signed up to compete in the 2009 season?

2. Which race in the 2009 tournament was abandoned due to heavy rain?

3. Who won the 2009 Monaco Grand Prix?

4. Which Grand Prix have been dropped in the 2009 tournament?

5. Who was the 2008 World Champion?

6. Which team pulled out in December 2008 and were re-branded as Brawn GP?

7. Which Grand Prix was the first to be held at night during the 2008 season?

8. Which famous driver was replaced at Toyota by Timo Glock in 2008?

9. What is the name of the new 2009 Abu Dhabi GP track?

10. Which British TV company have the rights for coverage of the 2009 Formula One season?

11. Which team withdrew just four races into the 2008 championship due to financial troubles?

12. Which famous Scottish driver withdrew from the 2009 championship to become a TV anchor providing coverage of F1 for the BBC?

13. Which Japanese track has replaced Fuji Speedway for 2009?

14. Who won their third Grand Prix at Silverstone in 2009?

15. What is the average viewing figure for a race (globally)?
A) 500million B) 600million
C) 750million

16. Who holds the current record for the most consecutive GP wins?

17. Where are modern F1 car engines situated?

18. What is the name of the only Australian driver in the 2009 championship?

19. What did the Benetton team change its name to?

20. What is the oldest team currently competing in Formula One?

21. Where was Lewis Hamilton born?

22. What is the name of the driver who died during the first race at the San Marino GP?

23. What was the name of the first Formula One Championship winner?

24. How many litres is the current F1 car engine? A) 2.0 B) 24 C) 3.0

25. How much does one Formula One steering wheel cost? A) $21,000
B) $25,000 C) $31,000

Answers on pg 59

AWAY FROM THE TRACK

Ever wondered what the drivers do to relax when they're not racing? Here is the inside track on the hobbies and pastimes the fastest men on the planet enjoy when they are not behind the steering wheel…

Lewis Hamilton
The British driver who was the 2008 champion enjoys playing guitar, remote-control cars and online gaming. He is also interested in football and rumoured to be an Aston Villa supporter.

Heikki Kovalainen
The Finnish racer is a keen skier, cyclist and golfer but he also plays video games in his spare time.

Felipe Massa
Massa is a movie buff and regularly attends gala premieres – or pops down to his local cinema with his wife Rafaela. Being Brazilian, it's no surprise he also plays football.

Kimi Räikkönen
Kimi likes all sports that involve some sort of boarding – but his favourites are skateboarding and snowboarding.

Robert Kubica
Robert started out in go-karting and still competes today but he also likes tenpin bowling and video games.

Nick Heidfeld
Nick recently got engaged to his long-term girlfriend Patricia and likes all sports, music, cinema and cars but he also has an interest in motorcycles.

Fernando Alonso
Fernando likes all sport and films but loves computers and football in particular.

Jarno Trulli
The Italian racer still competes in karting – old habits die hard! - but he also loves music, cinema, computers and video games.

Timo Glock
Timo likes to do all sports and like his team-mates, is still involved with karting.

Sébastien Buemi
The young Swiss driver enjoys tennis and golf.

Mark Webber
Mark likes remote-control planes and playing his PS3.

Sebastian Vettel
Sebastian is a keen swimmer and loves snowboarding too.

Nico Rosberg
The son of world champion Keke Rosberg enjoys playing football, snowboarding and jet-skiing.

Kazuki Nakajima
The Japanese driver plays a lot of football and likes listening to music.

Adrian Sutil
Adrian can play piano but also enjoys snooker and pool.

Giancarlo Fisichella
Giancarlo plays football, tennis and pool but he is also a keen fisherman – must be something to do with his surname!

Jenson Button
Jenson is a keen shopper and enjoys video games.

Rubens Barrichello
The Brazilian driver is still involved with his karting roots but he also enjoys golf and tenpin bowling.

Jaime Alguersuari
The yougest driver in F1 history enjoys karting, golf and tennis.

HEIKKI KOVALAINEN

Team: McLaren
Born: 19/10/1981
Nationality: Finnish
Birthplace: Suomussalmi, Finland
World Championships: 0
Highest Finish: 1
Race Wins: 1

SÉBASTIEN BUEMI

Team: Toro Rosso
Born: 31/10/1988
Nationality: Swiss
Birthplace: Aigle, Switzerland
World Championships: 0
Highest Finish: 7
Race Wins: 0

ROBERT KUBICA

Team: BMW Sauber
Born: 07/12/1984
Nationality: Polish
Birthplace: Krakow, Poland
World Championships: 0
Highest Finish: 1
Race Wins: 1

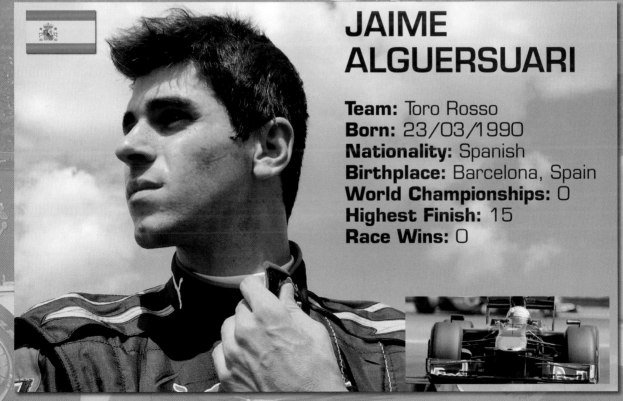

JAIME ALGUERSUARI

Team: Toro Rosso
Born: 23/03/1990
Nationality: Spanish
Birthplace: Barcelona, Spain
World Championships: 0
Highest Finish: 15
Race Wins: 0

DETAILS CORRECT TO 31/07/09

SPOT THE DIFFERENCE

Picture A and B are the same – or are they? Can you spot and circle the six differences in Picture B?

Answers on pg 58

WHICH CIRCUIT ?

Can you solve the puzzle of the mystery circuits below – use your powers of observation to pick up on the clues within the picture...

F1 AROUND THE WORLD

2009 DRIVER LINE-UP

FRONT ROW: (Left to Right)
Nick Heidfeld (Germany), Robert Kubica (Poland) of BMW Sauber, Felipe Massa (Brazil), Kimi Räikkönen (Finland) of Ferrari, Lewis Hamilton (Britain), Heikki Kovalainen (Finland) of McLaren Mercedes, Fernando Alonso (Spain) of Renault, Nelsinho Piquet (Brazil) – withdrawn from Renault, Aug 2009

ING AUSTRALIAN GRAND PRIX

MELBOURNE 2009

ITALIAN GRAND PRIX

MONZA CIRCUIT, MONZA

First Race: 1950
Circuit Length: 5.760 Km
Laps: 53
Built: 1950
Capacity: 115,000

SINGAPORE

MARINA BAY, SINGAPORE

First Race: 2008
Circuit Length: 5.037 Km
Laps: 61
Built: 2008 (street circuit)
Capacity: 100,000

JAPANESE GRAND PRIX

SUZUKA INTERNATIONAL RACING COURSE, SUZUKA

First Race: 1987
Circuit Length: 5.773 Km
Laps: 53
Built: 1962
Capacity: 100,000

BRAZILIAN GRAND PRIX

AUTODROMO JOSE CARLOS PACE, SAO PAOLO

First Race: 1973
Circuit Length: 4.283 Km
Laps: 71
Built: 1940
Capacity: 80,000

HELMET QUIZ

Can you guess which driver is beneath the helmet? There are clues if you look hard enough...

Answers on pg 59

ABU DHABI

YAS MARINA CIRCUIT – YAS ISLAND, ABU DHABI

First race: 2009
Circuit length: 5.522 km
Laps: 55
Built: 2009
Capacity: 41,093

OFFDUTY
Behind the scenes with the stars of Formula One

Jenson Button

Lewis Hamilton

Mark Webber

Nick Heidfeld

Timo Glock

CRASHBANGWALLOP!
When Formula One goes wrong...

1) David Coulthard of Red Bull and Japanese Kazuki Nakajima of Williams are involved in an accident after the start of the Formula One Grand Prix in Brazil in July 2008.

1

2) Giancarlo Fisichella of Italy is lifted out of turn ten after a crash during the third practice session on the Marina Bay City Circuit in Singapore, 27th September 2008.

2

3) Britain's David Coulthard, right, Red Bull, and Germany's Sebastian Vettel, crash out at the Priory corner in the British Grand Prix at Silverstone, England, 6th July 2008.

3

4) Nico Rosberg's car is lifted up after a crash during the Monaco Grand Prix, 25th May 2008.

4

SAFETY CAR

The Formula One Safety Car is immediately on hand whenever the safety of the race is threatened by accidents, adverse weather or other hazardous situations. It can limit the speed of competing cars on a racetrack during a caution period during which the Safety Car enters the track ahead of the leader.

With few exceptions, competitors are not allowed to pass the Safety Car or other competitors during a caution period, and the Safety Car leads the field at a predetermined safe speed, which may vary by series and circuit. At the end of the caution period, the Safety Car leaves the track and the competitors may resume racing.

The 2009 Safety Car is the new SL 63 AMG with a 6.3 litre V8 engine producing 525hp with a 0-62mph time of 4.6 seconds (for all you petrol-heads out there!). With Germany's expert driver Bernd Mayländer behind the wheel, the Safety Car will be able to stay in front of some of the world's fastest racing drivers guiding them around the circuit.

Safety Car rules were changed for the 2009 season. The previous regulations, which saw the pit lane closed for a period of time after the Safety Car's deployment, came under intense scrutiny last year after several drivers were penalised for pitting to avoid running out of fuel.

The revisions for 2009 will see the pit lane remain open at all times. But to prevent drivers rushing back to the pits - the reason for the original rule change - a new electronic system, which uses the standard engine control unit (ECU), will be implemented.

GIANCARLO FISICHELLA

Team: Force India
Born: 14/01/1973
Nationality: Italian
Birthplace: Rome, Italy
World Championships: 0
Highest Finish: 1
Race Wins: 3

ADRIAN SUTIL

Team: Force India
Born: 11/01/1983
Nationality: German
Birthplace: Starnberg, Germany
World Championships: 0
Highest Finish: 8
Race Wins: 0

KAZUKI NAKAJIMA

Team: Williams
Born: 11/01/1985
Nationality: Japanese
Birthplace: Aichi, Japan
World Championships: 0
Highest Finish: 6
Race Wins: 0

DETAILS CORRECT TO 31/07/09

QUIZANSWERS

CIRCUIT BREAKER QUIZ ANSWERS (PG 20)

1 Bahrain (1)

2 Singapore

3 Abu Dhabi

4 Bahrain (2)

5 Australia

6 Monaco

7 China

8 Malaysia

SPOT THE DIFFERENCE ANSWERS (PG 42)
Did you find all six changes in Picture B?

SPOT THE DIFFERENCE ANSWERS (PG 15)
Did you find all six changes in Picture B?

GUESS WHO?
ANSWERS (PG 25)

1 Jenson Button at the Goodwood Festival of Speed

2 Sebastian Vettel after winning the British Grand Prix

3 Jarno Trulli

4 Kimi Räikkönen loses control in Bahrain back in 2006

```
K N A T L E U F Y R
E L E C T R I C A L
B T S G A R D L R W
E S B R A K E S   H
K U R K D H E K R E
B A Y V W N Z N P E
L H T R I O R C L L
Z X M G L S N T T S
D E N J E K K G J C
C E Z G K N T Y F Q
```

▲ **WORDSEARCH SOLUTION (PG 34)**

```
            A              S
            P      P I T    T
         T W E N T Y   E    R
            X    A Y R T O N E E N
            O    R        E
            N    H A M I L T O N
      J E N S O N    N
              F      T      B
        F    U       I      R   E
        R  C H E Q U E R E D A   N
        R  I      L  C      Z   G
        A  R      Q U A L I F Y I N
        R  C      U  R      L   N
        A  U    H E L M E T O    E
        R  I
      L I G H T S
```

▲ **CROSSWORD SOLUTION (PG 28)**

THE**BIG**
F1**QUIZ**

ANSWERS FROM (PGS 36&37)

1	TEN
2	MALAYSIAN GRAND PRIX
3	JENSON BUTTON
4	FRANCE AND CANADA
5	LEWIS HAMILTON
6	HONDA
7	2008 SINGAPORE GP
8	RALF SCHUMACHER
9	YAS MARINA CIRCUIT
10	BBC
11	SUPER AGURI
12	DAVID COULTHARD
13	SUZUKA CIRCUIT
14	SEBASTIAN VETTEL
15	B) 600 MILLION PEOPLE GLOBALLY
16	MICHAEL SCHUMACHER
17	IN THE MIDDLE
18	MARK WEBBER
19	RENAULT
20	FERRARI
21	STEVENAGE
22	AYRTON SENNA
23	NINO FARINA
24	B) 24 LITRES
25	C) $31,000

WHICH CIRCUIT QUIZ
ANSWERS (PG 43)

1 Silverstone

2 Istanbul

3 Singapore

4 Monte Carlo

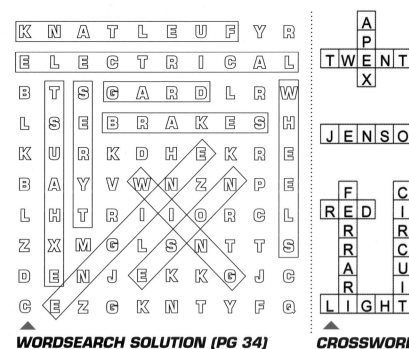

HELMET QUIZ
ANSWERS (PG 50)

1 Sebastian Vettel

2 Lewis Hamilton

3 Mark Webber

4 Fernando Alonso

page59

YEAR	CHAMPIONS	CONSTRUCTORS
2008	Lewis HAMILTON (GBR)	Ferrari
2007	Kimi RAIKKONEN (FIN)	Ferrari
2006	Fernando ALONSO (SPA)	Renault
2005	Fernando ALONSO (SPA)	Renault
2004	Michael SCHUMACHER (GER)	Ferrari
2003	Michael SCHUMACHER (GER)	Ferrari
2002	Michael SCHUMACHER (GER)	Ferrari
2001	Michael SCHUMACHER (GER)	Ferrari
2000	Michael SCHUMACHER (GER)	Ferrari
1999	Mika HAKKINEN (FIN)	Ferrari
1998	Mika HAKKINEN (FIN)	McLaren - Mercedes
1997	Jacques VILLENEUVE (CAN)	Williams - Renault
1996	Damon HILL (GBR)	Williams - Renault
1995	Michael SCHUMACHER (GER)	Benetton - Renault
1994	Michael SCHUMACHER (GER)	Williams - Renault
1993	Alain PROST (FRA)	Williams - Renault
1992	Nigel MANSELL (GBR)	Williams - Renault
1991	Ayrton SENNA (BRA)	McLaren - Honda
1990	Ayrton SENNA (BRA)	McLaren - Honda
1989	Alain PROST (FRA)	McLaren - Honda
1988	Ayrton SENNA (BRA)	McLaren - Honda
1987	Nelson PIQUET (BRA)	Williams - Honda
1986	Alain PROST (FRA)	Williams - Honda
1985	Alain PROST (FRA)	McLaren - TAG/Porsche
1984	Niki LAUDA (AUT)	McLaren - TAG/Porsche
1983	Nelson PIQUET (BRA)	Ferrari
1982	Keke ROSBERG (FIN)	Ferrari
1981	Nelson PIQUET (BRA)	Williams - Ford/Cosworth
1980	Alan JONES (AUS)	Williams - Ford/Cosworth
1979	Jody SCHECKTER (SAF)	Ferrari
1978	Mario ANDRETTI (USA)	Lotus - Ford/Cosworth
1977	Niki LAUDA (AUT)	Ferrari
1976	James HUNT (GBR)	Ferrari
1975	Niki LAUDA (AUT)	Ferrari
1974	Emerson FITTIPALDI (BRA)	McLaren - Ford/Cosworth
1973	Jackie STEWART (GBR)	Lotus - Ford/Cosworth
1972	Emerson FITTIPALDI (BRA)	Lotus - Ford/Cosworth
1971	Jackie STEWART (GBR)	Tyrrell - Ford/Cosworth
1970	Jochen RINDT (AUT)	Lotus - Ford/Cosworth
1969	Jackie STEWART (GBR)	Matra - Ford/Cosworth
1968	Graham HILL (GBR)	Lotus - Ford/Cosworth
1967	Denny HULME (NZL)	Brabham - Repco
1966	Jack BRABHAM (AUS)	Brabham - Repco
1965	Jim CLARK (GBR)	Lotus - Climax
1964	John SURTEES (GBR)	Ferrari
1963	Jim CLARK (GBR)	Lotus - Climax
1962	Graham HILL (GBR)	BRM
1961	Phil HILL (USA)	Ferrari
1960	Jack BRABHAM (AUS)	Cooper - Climax
1959	Jack BRABHAM (AUS)	Cooper - Climax
1958	Mike HAWTHORN (GBR)	Vanwall
1957	Juan Manuel FANGIO (ARG)	
1956	Juan Manuel FANGIO (ARG)	
1955	Juan Manuel FANGIO (ARG)	
1954	Juan Manuel FANGIO (ARG)	
1953	Alberto ASCARI (ITA)	
1952	Alberto ASCARI (ITA)	
1951	Juan Manuel FANGIO (ARG)	
1950	Giuseppe "Nino" FARINA (ITA)